T0021265

INSPIRING GUIDES

Calm

100 Affirmations for Serenity

Elicia Rose

ROCK
POINT

Thank you to my family, who have always encouraged me to dream big and have supported me every step of the way.

Contents

Introduction

Inner peace—the elusive concept that everyone seems to want to attain. Throughout the ages, people from every walk of life have tried to find peace within themselves. Ask a mystic, a meditation teacher, or an average person and each will offer you their own ideas on what makes them feel calm and peaceful. The trouble is, we face more distractions and busier lives than ever before. To feel calm and grounded on a daily basis seems more of a luxury than a necessity.

It's no secret that most of us can feel overwhelmed to say the least. We find ourselves constantly plugged in, never taking a moment to simply stop and rest. Advances in technology offer us so many benefits, but it's easier than ever to spend all night scrolling on your phone, absorbing so much information from social media and the internet that your mind feels overwhelmed. We've all been there. Many of us know that we need to take some time to slow down, but how exactly do we do this?

My take on finding the calm within is that it isn't some lifelong journey that you need to pursue at all costs. I believe inner peace is cultivated through the habits and actions of our daily lives. As we start small and bring awareness to our current thoughts, feelings, and actions, we become mindful of what is helping our inner peace and what might hinder it. This starts by us becoming aware of how we speak to ourselves. Words are powerful, and if we find ourselves constantly critiquing or judging ourselves and our lives, then it's natural that our mood will reflect this. This is where I believe positive affirmations offer an antidote to stress and anxiety.

Positive affirmations are free, simple to use, and can help improve your mood in a matter of seconds. A simple definition of a positive affirmation is a statement written in the first person and ideally in the present tense that helps you cultivate a more balanced way of thinking. If you see yourself from an unhelpful frame of mind, positive affirmations can help address this by inviting in more self-acceptance, self-compassion, and clarity. With repetition and consistency, positive affirmations become an anchor for calm, peace, and serenity.

Bloom Affirmations, my business, was first created with the idea that sharing powerful tools like positive affirmations could help shape people's mind-sets for

the better. It started as an Instagram account where I could share inspiring content to help make social media a kinder place to be. As my self-development journey has continued, I now share a range of tools, products, and content, all with the aim of helping people feel better about themselves and find more inner calm. I continue to enjoy the benefits of positive affirmations, journaling, and meditation, and I know this is available for you too. This is why in this book you will find a hundred affirmations broken down into categories so you find inspiration and motivation in your everyday. You'll also find a reflection or an exercise accompanying each affirmation to help you incorporate more peace into your day.

In terms of how you use positive affirmations, you can choose any method that resonates with you. I recommend writing affirmations in your journal, then completing the accompanying journal prompt or exercise. Once you have done this, you can write or place the affirmation in a space where you will see it often throughout your day. You might set reminders on your phone or place a note on your desk. Another great idea is to change the wallpaper on your phone to your chosen affirmation(s), so that you are continually reminded of it. The more you work with your affirmations, the stronger they become. Positive affirmations are by no means the full solution in finding inner peace, but they are certainly a useful tool to help you feel calmer.

You can use this book in many ways. Feel free to read it through, or alternatively you might pick a page at random and receive guidance and inspiration for the day. Take your time with each affirmation and exercise and be mindful of what thoughts and feelings they bring up. This book is designed to calm, nourish, and restore your body and mind. The more time you put into each affirmation and exercise, the more you will feel the benefits.

Know that calm, peace, and serenity are always available to you, even in the busiest and most stressful of moments. We don't always have a choice about what happens in our environment, but we always have a choice over our inner landscape. You deserve to feel grounded, balanced, and blissful.

My hope is that this book acts as a warm, gentle hug, reminding you that you deserve to feel peaceful and calm, even when you don't feel that way. Allow your intuition to guide you to the affirmations and practices you need the most, and feel free to change the words of any affirmations so they resonate with you. Positive affirmations have had a huge impact on my mind-set, and I hope you will also feel their benefits.

Mindfulness

We all experience feelings of stress and tension, but most of these feelings go unnoticed as we move on autopilot through our busy days. When was the last time you checked in with yourself to see how you are actually feeling? In order to increase feelings of calm and serenity, we must first become present to fully understand what we are experiencing.

If you wish to change your current state, you need to get clear on your starting point. Most of us spend a lot of the time running away from how we truly feel. Simply allowing space for all thoughts and feelings without judgment is a powerful step in feeling calm.

We also tend to worry about things we can't control. It's easy to focus on things that have already happened or ruminate about what might happen in the future. This mind-set often keeps us in a loop of anxiety and stress. In reality, all we have is the present moment. Being mindful means staying connected to the present moment instead of worrying about things we cannot change.

No matter what thoughts or feelings you are experiencing, know that they will pass. Becoming mindful means becoming aware of the beautiful gift of being human. From this moment on, choose to meet whatever arises with love, understanding, and acceptance.

The following affirmations and exercises are designed to cultivate feelings of mindfulness and awareness, without trying to alter anything about your current experience.

I tune into the present moment

The present moment is all we ever really have, yet we barely spend any time here. We find ourselves caught up in thinking about the past or living in the future. Arriving in the here and now might seem strange at first, but one of the easiest ways to do this is to turn your attention to your environment.

Check in on your surroundings. Spend a few minutes observing everything around you. Write down five things you can see and include as much detail as possible.

The more mindful I am, the better I feel

As you begin your journey to become calmer and more peaceful, know that every time you decide to cultivate mindfulness, you're one step closer to making these feelings a lasting presence in your life.

Write a mindful mission statement. Declare that you are ready to begin this journey, and detail everything you would like to feel as you progress. Here's an example: I am ready to feel calmer, more peaceful, and more content. I am excited about learning to become mindful, and hope to experience more clarity as I progress.

I create space for all my thoughts and feelings

Creating space for thoughts and feelings might seem strange, but it's very simple. It's all about sitting with whatever you are thinking and feeling without any judgment or criticism. Simply allow your thoughts and feelings to arise, letting them flow through you. Pretty soon you will begin to notice their intensity drop.

Complete this sentence: In order for me to become more mindful on a daily basis, I will . . .

I anchor myself in the now

Our society loves to promote multitasking, but this often leaves us feeling unfocused as we swap between activities. Accomplishing one thing at a time allows our mind to focus and for the activity to become a mindful practice itself.

Today, try doing one activity without combining it with another. This might mean turning the radio off on your drive into work or leaving your headphones at home as you go on a walk. Focus solely on what you are doing and allow it to become a mindful practice.

I am grounded, present, and aware

There are areas of life where you will already experience being fully in the moment. Think about an activity that you love doing, where the time flies and you lose track of everything else. It might be catching up with friends, playing your favorite sport, or walking through a beautiful park.

In what areas of your life do you already enjoy being in the present moment?

I allow my breath to become my focus

We take thousands of breaths every day without paying much attention, but our breath can be used as a tool for connecting us back to our bodies. The breath is a great way of making us aware of the present moment.

Become mindful of your breath for a few moments. Note anything you observe about it. Is it fast or slow? Deep or shallow? Can you feel it most in the collarbone, chest, or stomach? After you've spent a few moments observing the breath, begin to gradually slow it down and take deeper breaths directed into the abdomen, if this feels comfortable. Continue breathing in this comfortable and relaxing way until you feel your whole body relax.

I have the power to change what doesn't serve me

As you become more mindful, you might notice thoughts that you weren't previously aware of. This is a great thing. Rather than ignoring them or numbing out, you now have the ability to process and feel them, letting go of what no longer serves you.

What thoughts do you find the most difficult to process or let go of? Why do you think this is?

I bring a loving awareness into every single cell of my body

When was the last time you became fully aware of all parts of your body? We don't tend to notice our bodies unless we experience pain or discomfort.

Do a body scan. Find a comfortable place where you won't be disturbed and get into a comfortable and supportive position. Close your eyes, slow your breath, and allow your body to relax. Begin to send your awareness to your feet, including your toes and ankles. Slowly work your way up the body, stopping in each part and sending your awareness there. Don't try to change any experiences you might notice. Simply observe them. Finish by sending awareness to the crown of your head.

I am here,
I am whole

You are whole and worthy exactly as you are. You aren't lacking in anything and you don't need to fix yourself. We all possess an inherent worthiness simply because we exist. You don't need to earn it. All you need to do is integrate the belief that you are already enough.

Practice this body mindfulness exercise. What parts of your body do you feel the least connected to? Why do you think this is? Are you able to bring a loving and accepting awareness to these parts of your body?

I give myself the space to experience all of my thoughts and feelings

Give yourself space to experience whatever comes up during your daily life with love and acceptance. Release the resistance and let yourself be exactly as you are.

Do this daily habit-builder exercise. Set a reminder on your phone three times a day with the title "Mindfulness check-in." When you see this notification, bring awareness to how you are feeling, what you are thinking, and any other sensations you might notice within your body. Don't try to change them; simply let them be.

I am grateful for the gift of connecting to my heart

Try this exercise for expanding your heart center and filling yourself up with feelings of warmth, compassion, and love.

Sit upright with your spine straight yet relaxed. Begin to slow and deepen your breath. Place your hands in a prayer position in front of your heart. Imagine a glowing golden energy beginning to form at your heart center. With each breath, see this beautiful energy grow stronger. As you inhale, imagine this energy expanding into a bubble that includes your whole body. As you exhale, imagine this energy returning to your heart. Visualize this energy expanding and contracting like your lungs do. Spend a few moments feeling your heart center open and strengthen, visualizing the bubble expanding as wide as it needs to.

I greet resistance with love and kindness

Resistance is normal, natural, and part of life. It can be felt when things don't turn out as we'd hoped, as tension in relationships, or even as inner resistance when we go through tough times. We will experience it within ourselves, with others, and during all phases of life. How we choose to approach it, however, is up to us. A good place to start noticing resistance is by identifying it within our own body.

Close your eyes and begin to tune into your body. Where are you currently holding tension or experiencing any tightness or discomfort? Once you have identified these areas, begin sending a light and spacious breath to each part until you feel some tension begin to release.

I inhale awareness and exhale judgment

We always have the capacity to stop what we are doing, become aware, and choose a more grounding and calming way to approach things. Visual or physical reminders, along with the breath, are great tools for accomplishing this.

Create an anchor that will guide you to the present moment and remind you to check in with how you are feeling. This might be a symbol, a picture, or another visual prompt, but it could also be a simple physical movement, such as gently squeezing your wrist or tapping your thumb against the tips of your fingers. Experiment until you find one that feels right, then write it down in your journal. Try using this throughout the day to bring yourself back to the present moment.

I invite spaciousness into my body

We often go about our days with so much tension, frustration, or discomfort that it can be really relaxing to intentionally invite spaciousness into the body. To me, spaciousness means an unraveling of anything tight that we have been holding on to and expanding into a peaceful state.

Make friends with uncomfortable feelings with this visualization technique. Sit upright with your shoulders and jaw relaxed. Take a few deep, slow breaths, and close your eyes. Allow a few moments to observe your breath and begin to settle. Imagine an unpleasant feeling that you have been experiencing a lot recently and visualize it in a human, animal, or object form. Keep it abstract and don't link it to anything or anyone that you love. Begin to beam loving and accepting feelings to this personified emotion. When you feel ready, visualize hugging the emotion and accepting it for what it is.

It is safe for me to arrive in this moment

Sometimes the idea of sitting with our thoughts or feelings might seem strange or uncomfortable at first, and that's okay. The more we practice, the better we become at it. It can be helpful to explore why you struggle with the present moment to gain a better understanding of how you can make peace with it.

Complete this sentence: Sometimes I find it difficult to be in the present moment because . . .

I have the ability to create my own world

You are a powerful being, and you have the ability to shape how you see the world around you. You can listen to other narratives and adopt them as your own, or you can choose to create your own world.

Think about how you see the world around you. Is this your own narrative, or have you been listening to external voices? Journal about the world you would like to live in.

I let my daily worries melt away and focus on the here and now

Cultivating mindfulness after a busy day is a great way to process what you might have experienced and make sense of what happened. It can help make your evenings more peaceful and relaxing and improve your sleep quality.

At the end of the day, journal the predominant feelings you have experienced throughout the day. Once you have written them down, label their intensity (10 being the most intense and 1 being barely noticeable). For each feeling you have listed, write down the possible causes. This is a great way to begin cultivating mindfulness around your emotional state and how it varies throughout the day.

I bring awareness to parts of myself that I may have once hidden away

As you begin practicing mindfulness, you might notice parts of yourself you used to hide away. Be kind to yourself as you begin to reflect on these things.

Make a list of the parts of yourself you used to hide away but that you are now becoming more aware of. Why do you think you didn't pay attention to these things before? What can you do to become more accepting of them?

I cultivate the habit of becoming present in the now

Our phones can be one of the biggest barriers to being present, so it's a good idea to rethink our device usage.

Practice no-phone time. I invite you to turn off notifications from all the apps you use the most and get into the habit of leaving your phone in another room. You can begin by doing this for an hour every evening, eventually building up to a full day every week. If you're waiting for important calls or messages, you can put your phone in another room but leave it on loud. See how this affects your levels of productivity and inner peace.

I see this present moment as a gift

The here and now is all we ever really have, and when we find ourselves fully present in the moment, it helps to reflect on these experiences. Take some time today to practice being fully present and see how it feels. Spend some time outside, read a book, play with your kids or pets, or engage in another activity that requires your full attention. You might just find that life offers you gifts every single day.

Journal about a moment where you felt the most present and engaged today. What were you doing? How did it feel? Did it make you feel grateful for your life?

Being in the present moment comes easily and naturally to me

Becoming mindful doesn't need to be something that is difficult to attain or hard to work at. Of course, it requires some practice, but it is completely possible that it will come naturally to you after some time.

Think about some of the skills you possess today. They might have been learned at work, school, through a hobby, or other areas of life. Did they seem difficult at first? How did you develop these skills and what did you learn along the way?

I allow difficult thoughts or feelings to pass by without attachment

Imagine your thoughts and feelings are like clouds. You can lie on the grass and watch them float by without paying too much attention to any specific one.

Do an automatic writing exercise. Grab your pen and some paper or your journal and begin to write whatever comes to mind. Don't think too much about what you are writing, simply allow it to flow. Don't worry about what it sounds like or whether it even makes sense. This is a great exercise for letting go of thoughts and feelings and becoming mindful of your current state.

I know that this too shall pass

Nothing lasts forever, including both good and bad experiences. No matter how painful something is, take comfort in the fact that eventually the feelings will dissipate. Equally, if you're experiencing something wonderful, make sure you enjoy every moment.

Journal about a time where you recently decided to cultivate mindfulness and really live in the moment. Explore how it felt and the sensations you experienced. Once you have identified the event, complete this sentence: I am proud of myself because . . .

I take each day as it comes, without fear or judgment

We don't have to take life so seriously, and we don't have to only engage in activities that are deemed productive or effective. Playfulness is a great way of living in the moment and letting the worries of everyday life slip away.

Enjoy a playful activity. This might include a game night with your family or friends, playing with your kids or pet, or even playing your favorite music and dancing in your kitchen. Allow yourself to be silly and express yourself freely.

As I surrender here in this present moment, all is well

If you have made the decision to invite more mindfulness, presence, and awareness into your life, you should be very proud of yourself. The journey to become a calmer and more grounded person isn't always easy, but it's always worth it.

What does being present mean to you? Has this definition changed, and if so, how has it changed? Reflect on this in your journal and consider writing your own definition.

Calm &
Ground

Now that we've focused on arriving in the present moment and bringing awareness to how we feel, we can begin to cultivate feelings of calmness. To me, calmness means feeling balanced and grounded within myself. Tension leaves my body, my mind quiets, and everything feels peaceful.

Feelings of calm and serenity are much easier to access than you might think. It only takes a few moments to notice how you are feeling and decide to invite feelings of peace into the mind and body. We might not always be able to control our external environment, but we do have the power to change how we think and feel.

Think about your favorite way to relax. For me, this is lying on a beach and reading a good book. If I spend a few moments visualizing this scene, I'll notice my breath begin to slow and my shoulders relax. Nothing has changed in my surroundings, but mentally, I'm in a whole other place.

Learning to ground ourselves is also an important factor in feeling calm. When we are stressed or anxious, we can often feel like we aren't quite in our body. If we find ourselves with a racing mind, this disconnection from the body grows, and it can be easy to be swayed and pulled in any direction.

To me, grounding means to become present within my body or connecting to my inner roots. It can also mean connecting with your breath.

The following affirmations and exercises are designed to help you feel calm, grounded, and peaceful as you find and connect to your inner anchor.

As I go deeper within myself, I am able to find an inner stillness

I believe we can all access feelings of calm, no matter what we have experienced or what is happening around us. Before we begin to cultivate more of these feelings, it's helpful to reflect on when we've felt like this in the past.

When do you feel the most calm and grounded? Journal about these experiences or activities and how they make you feel.

I connect with my inner anchor to find peace and clarity

There is a place inside all of us where stillness exists. Nature can really help us connect to this place.

Practice this grounding meditation. Go to your favorite place in nature and take your shoes off, if possible. If this isn't an option, find a cozy space in your house and play your favorite nature music. Spend a few moments feeling the ground beneath your feet, or visualize standing barefoot. Close your eyes and direct your breath down to your feet. Once you begin to feel your body relax, visualize roots beginning to grow from your feet deep down into the earth. With each breath, see the roots grow deeper and thicker. Know that you are deeply connected to the stable and solid earth beneath you.

I am safe, calm, and grounded

This affirmation is the one I turn to when I feel myself getting stressed or unsettled. It reminds me that no matter what I am experiencing, I am going to be okay. If you don't feel safe, then it's very hard to feel calm and relaxed. When do you feel the safest? What helps you feel safe?

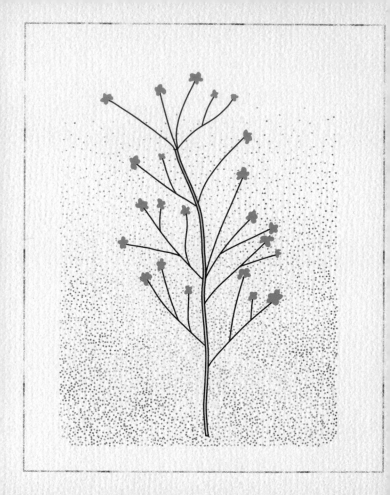

I invite stillness into my mind and body

Learning to self-soothe is a powerful skill to cultivate. One way we can do this is through physical touch. We might look for affection from others, but have you ever considered offering it to yourself?

Do a self-massage. Gently rub your index and middle fingers in circular motions over your forehead, temples, cheekbones, and along your jaw. Close your eyes and enjoy the feeling of tension melting away. Rub any tension away from your shoulders, arms, or anywhere else that feels tight. You can also use a soothing essential oil or moisturiser for extra relaxation. If you are using an essential oil or moisturizer, please test a small part of your skin or ask your doctor before using.

I cultivate calming and peaceful thoughts

Picture your mind like a beautiful garden. The most beautiful plants and flowers don't grow there by accident. They have been planted, nurtured, and lovingly tended to. The weeds that threaten their growth have been removed, and every effort has been made to allow them to thrive.

Make a list of some of your most common recurring thoughts, both positive and negative. Which ones deserve more attention, and which ones don't need feeding as much?

I choose to have a peaceful day

You have so much more power than you realize. Consider using this affirmation as part of your morning routine or writing it on a sticky note and placing it on your bedside table.

Complete this sentence: In order for me to feel grounded and at peace on a daily basis, I will . . .

I inhale peace and exhale tension

The reason why I love breathwork is that it's simple, free, quick, and easily accessible, no matter where I am.

When you make your exhalations longer than your inhalations, it has a calming and restorative effect on your body. Try inhaling for a count of four and exhaling for a count of six to eight, if this feels comfortable. Continue this pattern of breathing for a few minutes. Listen to your body and always stop if you feel lightheaded.

I am grounded and rooted to my authentic self

Your authentic self is who you are at your core. We connect with this part of ourselves when we stop judging ourselves and worrying about what others think of us.

Spending some time alone is a great way to connect to your authentic self and figure out what really matters to you. Find a meditation or journaling spot and begin spending time there regularly. This might be a corner of your living room, your garden, a local park, or your favorite forest.

Today, I choose to feel balanced and peaceful

Although thoughts and feelings can be so strong it feels like they have full control over us, we can always choose again. We might not be able to choose to feel peaceful right away, but we can make the choice to be more open to it.

Practice this calming meditation. Find a place where you won't be disturbed and can fully relax. Close your eyes, relax your body, and begin to slow your breath. As you deepen your breath, feel any tension in your face, jaw, and shoulders dissolve. Begin to focus on your breath even more. As you inhale, visualize breathing in a calming, blue energy. Allow this energy to circulate through your entire body and fill up every cell. As you exhale, visualize any stress or tension leaving your body in a dark and sticky color. Keep visualizing this breath until you feel grounded.

I protect my energy and only allow in that which is loving and uplifting

If you're highly sensitive, it's pretty easy to pick up on all the stimuli around you and feel overwhelmed. Try practicing the following visualization at the start of your day to keep you grounded. Take a moment to visualize a bubble of healing and protective energy forming around your entire body in your favorite color. Imagine that this bubble only allows through energy that is loving. Any energy that is unwanted or not in alignment simply deflects off the bubble.

As I relax, my body naturally releases stress

Your body is wise and knows exactly what to do in times of stress and uncertainty. Sometimes all we need to do is take a step back and let our body balance and restore itself.

Write a thank you letter to your body for all it does to keep you alive. Thank the billions of cells working right now to keep you healthy, your heart for beating consistently, your lungs for breathing in the air around you, and any other parts that come to mind. Express gratitude for the automated processes that allow you to live and thrive.

I find peace and grounding in the solid and supportive earth beneath me

We are part of nature, yet we often forget this. Many of us live our lives indoors, surrounded by bright lights and synthetic materials, not really paying much attention to the world that exists beyond our windows. It's time to explore spending more time outdoors and your connection to nature.

What is your relationship to nature? Do you enjoy spending time outdoors? What can you do to deepen your connection with this planet?

I am safe,
I am supported,
I am serene

Let's take it back to the basics. Make the decision right now in this moment to affirm a state of complete trust, relaxation, and serenity.

Write the word "serenity" in your journal. What does this mean to you? Make a list of all the ways you have experienced this feeling and all the ways you can incorporate more of it into your daily life.

I have more power over my emotions than I realize

Emotions can feel so strong that it might seem impossible to alter them. In reality, we are much more powerful than we know. Even in the midst of a strong emotional reaction, we have the power to choose more helpful and productive feelings.

What emotions do you struggle with, or that seem to take over you? What are the triggers for these emotions? What would be a more productive way of reacting that would bring more peace to yourself and others?

I welcome feelings of relaxation and contentment

Choosing to feel content despite what might be happening around you is an effective way of standing in your personal power. You don't have to kid yourself that you're super happy, but deciding to be content can save a lot of emotional energy.

What are the benefits of feeling calm and grounded and how would cultivating these feelings impact your daily life?

I invite a relaxing and grounding energy to wash over me

If you're trying to feel calm during a stressful situation, it can help to recall a memory of complete and utter peace. It might be remembering a particularly relaxing vacation, a beautiful hike, or anything else that makes you feel happy.

When was a time in your life that you felt the most relaxed, grounded, and at peace?

I allow stress and tension to melt away with every breath

When we're stressed, our breath tends to be faster and shallower. Belly breathing takes a bit of practice, but it's so relaxing.

Get comfortable in a supported seated position or lie down if you wish. Close your eyes if comfortable and place your hands on your lower abdomen. Begin to turn your attention to your breath. As you relax, begin to direct your breath down to your stomach. Breathe in for a count of four to six and feel your belly expand in your hands. Don't try to force it and make sure you remain relaxed. Keep directing your breath down to your belly, breathing deep and slow. Exhale fully from your belly for a count of four to six, allowing your hands to return closer to your body. Continue this practice for a few minutes to feel calm and peaceful.

I know that calmness is available to me whenever I choose

Making time to relax and unwind is so important to all aspects of our health. We can access feelings of calm throughout the day, or we can also engage in our favorite relaxing activities at the end of a long and busy day.

Baths are a great way to relax and unwind. Make an occasion out of it. Light some candles, add some bath salts, and play some relaxing music. Allow your whole body to relax and your nervous system to reset. Or, alternatively, make a big deal about one of your favorite things to do. Do a mini celebration or make it a big event for yourself, light some candles, buy yourself flowers, play some music, etc.

As I see calm and peace available to others, I know that it is also available to me

We can find sources of inspiration all around us. From our loved ones to people we may follow on social media, we can always find others who embody a calm and peaceful energy.

Think of a person who is calm and grounded. How do they act? What qualities characterize them? How can you use them as a role model for implementing more calmness in your life?

My natural state is one of equilibrium

Some stress is natural and to be expected in our daily lives, but have you ever considered that your natural state, and the one your mind and body are always trying to return to, is a state of equilibrium?

How much stress do you feel on a daily basis? Is it possible to make any changes that would mitigate some of this stress?

Peacefulness is mine to claim

Peace and calm are yours to claim. You deserve it. Make the decision with confidence to claim these feelings for yourself. They aren't elusive and unattainable concepts. They are already available to you, if you decide to claim them.

Complete this sentence: I decide to claim peace and calm from this day onward because . . .

I invite calmness to have a ripple effect on my entire life

Feeling calmer will benefit you the most, but it will certainly benefit your loved ones too. A calmer relationship with yourself leads to a calmer relationship with others.

If you felt calmer and more grounded, how would this impact your close relationships? Make a list of your most important relationships and how they would benefit you if you were able to feel calmer and more relaxed.

I look to nature for feelings of calm and balance

Sometimes the answers to our problems are very simple and are found in the most beautiful of places. We might not even need words, or explanation. A sunset says it all. Nature works in perfect harmony; every cold winter is followed by a hopeful spring.

What lessons has nature taught you about calmness, serenity, or balance?

I deserve to feel at peace

You deserve to experience inner peace and tranquillity. You deserve to tend to yourself like you would a child, making sure all your needs are met. You deserve to rest and recuperate, simply because.

Buy a houseplant. Spend time cultivating it and watching it grow. I love tending to my indoor rose plant because it brings me so much happiness to watch it bloom. As you care for this plant, know that you too are worthy of love and care.

I embrace loving, peaceful, grounding energy

The work you have done in this section has hopefully left you feeling calmer, grounded, and more at peace with yourself. Don't worry if you don't feel like you're fully embodying these qualities just yet. Be patient with yourself as you make positive changes.

Think about where you were one week, one month, or one year ago. What have you learned about yourself? Reflect on how far you've come in learning how to calm and ground yourself.

An integral part of cultivating feelings of calm is the ability to release what no longer serves us. We often carry thoughts, feelings, and behaviors that we know aren't for our highest good, but they feel familiar, so they outstay their welcome.

To choose to release these things requires a lot of bravery. It often requires taking a leap into the unknown and making space for a different way of being. Deep down, we know it's the right thing to do, no matter how painful it might seem. When we choose to release negativity, both physically and mentally, we will eventually experience a deep sense of inner peace, knowing we have made the right choice. It might not always be easy, but you're not here to play small and stay confined to the same repetitive behaviors.

We also need to go from witnessing the resistance to releasing with love and compassion. Change isn't always easy, and it can require a lot of conscious effort, but deep inner peace comes from knowing you have let go of what no longer serves you.

The following affirmations and exercises are designed to help you identify what you are holding on to, both physically and mentally, that needs releasing. Take your time and meet any resistance with an open heart and mind.

I release any negative thoughts about myself and replace them with loving ones

Our inner critic can be a difficult voice to quiet, but with practice and patience, we can learn to let this voice become a small whisper, barely audible compared to the loving and supportive part within us.

Write down the critical thoughts you have about yourself. Then cross each of them out, writing next to each, "This is no longer my story."

I let go of
anything that
no longer
serves me

Now that you have reflected on critical thoughts, let's think about behaviors or actions that aren't currently serving you. This might include habits that you know don't make you feel good. We all have them, and this isn't the time to get critical about them. It's time to be honest about what might need to go.

What behaviors are currently not serving you?

I have the capacity to shape my life for the better

Shaping your life for the better begins slowly, then before you know it, you've made some pretty amazing changes. Others can't make these changes for you. It's all about understanding your own capacity and putting it into action.

What kind of changes would you like to make in your life?

I release any behaviors that no longer support my health and happiness

Cultivating an open and nonjudgmental attitude toward making change means you are ready to begin considering options you might have been closed off to before. Deep down, are you open to making positive, lasting change that improves your well-being and inner peace? If not, why do you feel resistance?

Criticism is no longer my story. I choose to cultivate compassion instead

Think about it: when has criticism ever made you feel better or led to anything productive? It's much more helpful (and effective) to meet the things you wish to change with an open mind and a loving approach.

What do you currently critique or judge about yourself? Once you have written these down, next to each one, write, "I am willing to love and accept this part of myself. I release the need to critique or blame."

I shed old versions of myself in order to become the most authentic version of me

As we move through life, our ideas and beliefs will change. People might come and go, passion for things might grow and fade, and your identity will keep shifting as a result. It's okay to have big parts of your identity fade away to make room for newer ideas.

How does change make you feel? What kind of thoughts, feelings, and emotions does it bring up?

I cultivate an awareness of what I need to change

You might realize that quite a few changes need to be made in order to promote a more balanced and calmer life.

How does fear show up in your life? Do you feel ready to let it go?

I get to decide what optimal growth looks like for me

Growth and progress look different for every single person. Don't compare your version of progress to someone else's, or measure it against standards that other people have imposed upon you. Make changes for yourself, by yourself. What does your version of optimal growth look like?

As I let go of fearful thoughts and feelings, I welcome inner peace

The more you let go of fear and stress, the more space you create for growth, acceptance, and inner peace. It might be difficult to know where to start, but keep going. You already know what to do.

How would the most confident, grounded, and powerful version of you handle stress and tension?

The more I release, the calmer I feel

Sometimes it feels impossible not to worry about something. No matter how hard you try, you just can't get something out of your mind. Rather than fighting it, it can be a good idea to give your full attention to it, and then let it settle.

Instead of allowing worry and fear to take over your day, set a timer for two minutes and allow yourself to think all your anxious thoughts. Once the timer is up, decide to focus on something productive and move on with your day.

I release the pressure I put on myself and focus on cultivating feelings of acceptance

Choosing to release the pressures we put on ourselves and cultivate self-acceptance will bring a calming energy into every aspect of your life.

What pressure have you been putting on yourself? What have you been hoping to achieve with this? Is it possible for you to release these expectations?

As I release what no longer works for me, I feel lighter

Visualization can be the most effective way to begin the process of releasing what's no longer working. Write down all the pressure and expectations you currently feel in your life. Then get comfortable, preferably lying down, and close your eyes. Begin to visualize in your mind's eye a basket in front of you. Imagine taking each pressure you listed and placing it in an individual box. Continue placing all your fears, worries, and expectations into small boxes. Once you have done this, visualize placing each box into the basket. Once the basket is full, imagine it floating far away from you. Know that these expectations have been released and are no longer yours to carry.

I welcome positive, uplifting, and lasting change

Change doesn't have to be drastic and sudden. It might happen slowly, without you being aware of it. As you become more aware of what is causing a lot of stress in your life, you will be able to shape your life to include more calm.

What is the story you tell yourself around what causes stress in your life? Is it possible to rewrite this story?

I am boundless in my ability to grow and transform

You are capable of much more than you realize. You have the capacity to change your life for the better. You are already doing so well in taking these steps to feel calmer.

Practice transformational journaling. If you could completely transform your life, what would it look like? Take your time with this question and allow your imagination to run wild! Think big; no dream is too small.

It is safe for me to release the things that no longer serve me

It is okay to let go. It is okay to release. It is okay to surrender. It is okay if you feel scared. It is okay if you feel resistance. You can do this.

Try this shower meditation. Let the water run over you and visualize the water acting as both a mental and a physical purifier. Repeat this affirmation, either aloud or in your mind, and visualize the energy that no longer serves you washing down the drain.

I let go of my fears and worries with grace

Your breath is so much more than just a bodily process. We can survive weeks without food, but only a few minutes without the breath. Allow your breath to guide you through this affirmation and know that you're only one breath away from feeling calmer.

Do a self-love meditation. Find a place where you won't be disturbed and get into a comfortable and relaxed position. Turn your attention to your breath. Imagine breathing in a healing, loving, golden energy and repeat to yourself, "I inhale love." As you exhale, visualize a sticky, gray energy leaving your body and repeat to yourself, "I let go of my fears and worries." Keep breathing in this pattern until you feel peace and calm wash over you.

I am brave,
I am courageous,
I can do this

You've overcome difficult situations before, and you'll continue to overcome them throughout the rest of your life. We humans might not be great at many things, but we are certainly very resilient.

Recall a time where you recently demonstrated courage or bravery. Courage doesn't have to be grand gestures. It could be a time you overcame something small or said yes to something outside of your comfort zone. How did it feel? What did you learn about yourself?

As I change the way I think about myself, I feel calm and at peace

How you view yourself might have stayed the same since you were a child. We often pick up beliefs at a very young age about who we are, what we should be, and how we should act. It is okay to form a new identity for yourself.

Write a letter to your inner child, and give them the love and attention they deserve. Tell them everything they needed to hear, but never got the chance to.

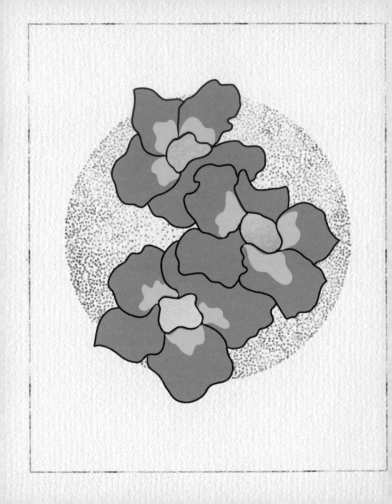

I release my limiting beliefs

The logical mind might think it's covered everything, but tune into your intuition. There might be some more insights that you hadn't considered before.

Write a letter to your higher self. Your higher self is your inner wisdom—the part of you that already knows the answers but is only accessed when you quiet your mind of worry and doubt. Light a candle and get your journal. Write at the top of the page, "Dear Highest Self, what do I need to release that I might not be aware of?" Take a few moments to tune in to how you're feeling and begin writing from the place of your intuition. Don't think too much about what you are writing, simply allow the words to flow.

I enjoy moving my body as a form of physical release

Taking care of our physical health is just as important as taking care of our mental health. In reality, the two are very much intertwined. Physical release is just as important as mental release. Burning off some energy can help you move through any resistance or tension.

Spend some time moving your body today in a way that feels good. This might include yoga, a short walk, or anything else that helps connect you back to your body.

I shift my energy to include feelings of peace, balance, and calm

A quick way to return to a calm state is to focus on saying and thinking nice things, especially about yourself. We might find this easier when thinking about others, but try thinking nice things about yourself.

Write down five loving thoughts and feelings you have toward yourself.

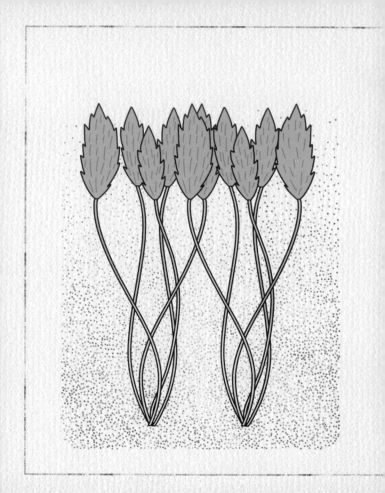

I let go of external pressures and use my intuition to guide me

Intuition is a powerful thing. We all know when something doesn't feel right but we can't explain it, or when something feels right even though it doesn't make sense. Spend some time listening to your intuition.

Journal about a time where your intuition was right about something. What physical sensations did you notice in your body? What kind of feelings did you have? What thoughts were prominent? Getting familiar with these sensations helps you identify your intuition when it speaks up in the future.

I release old stresses and worries. They are no longer my story

You always have the power to choose. In every moment you can choose to return to stress, or you can choose to remain grounded and let it pass by without attachment.

Practice this cleansing breath exercise. If you ever feel yourself getting stressed or overwhelmed, find a quiet place and begin focusing on your breath. Inhale deeply through the nose, and exhale loudly through the mouth. Sigh as loud as you can and make any noise that feels good. Even one minute of this breathing technique is enough to help you release tension.

I let go of who I think I should be in order to become who I truly am

Shake it out! You don't owe your worries anything. They don't need to weigh you down anymore.

Physically release any tension that you carry by dancing. Put on your favorite music and dance! Move your body as much as you can to work through any tension or stress that you might be holding.

I cleanse myself of anything I've picked up that doesn't support my inner peace

It's really important to physically cleanse the places in which we spend a lot of time. Places hold energy and can remind us of certain feelings.

Spend some time today cleaning your living or working space. Make sure you clean every single inch and throw or give away anything that no longer makes you feel good. Once you're done, light a candle or some incense, or open your windows to allow fresh air into the space.

Surrender

So far, we have cultivated mindfulness, invited calming and grounding energy into the mind and body, and released anything that no longer serves us. The next and final part in cultivating feelings of calmness and serenity is to fully surrender and learn to go with the flow of life.

To surrender doesn't mean giving up your personal power and dropping all ambitions and goals. Surrendering can be letting go of the idea that we always know what is best for us, and allowing life to gently lead us exactly where we need to go.

Although the mind is a wonderful asset that allows us to plan, imagine, and speculate, we can't possibly prepare for every single scenario that might unfold. This is the beauty and magic of life. If we always knew the end destination, the journey wouldn't be half as exciting.

To surrender means to flow effortlessly, like water. Every single raindrop eventually makes its way back to the vast oceans. We, too, will always end up exactly where we are meant to be. You might as well enjoy the journey and cherish the lessons rather than resist them.

The following affirmations and exercises are designed to help you surrender to the idea that we don't always know what comes next and that is okay.

I surrender and go with the flow of life

As much as we try to control life, life often has other plans for us. Imagine the wonderful things you might experience if you gave up control and trusted that everything will work out.

Make a prayer to a higher being that falls under your belief system: the Universe/God/Higher Self/Inner Knowing, etc. Dear (choose one that resonates or use your own), I surrender the idea that I know what is best for me, and I place my trust in you. I invite you to guide me toward whatever my soul needs for optimal growth while being grateful for the journey. Thank you for your unconditional love and support.

I embody the grace that already exists within me

You might not realize it yet, but you already embody grace and ease. It's not as unattainable as you might think.

How do you already embody ease and flow in your life? If you're struggling with this, think about the activities that come naturally to you without much effort.

I look to others for inspiration to teach me how to surrender

People are extraordinary, and everyone has the potential to teach others. We can look to others for guidance and inspiration, especially when they embody traits we wish to cultivate.

Who in your life demonstrates a deep trust and knowing that everything is going to work out? Make a list of them and what you admire about them. This can include people you know personally and people who inspire you. If you can't think of anyone, imagine what that person would look like, what actions they would take in tough situations, and what you would admire about them.

I trust that I am exactly where I need to be

What if where you are in life is exactly where you need to be? What if this part of your life could teach you valuable lessons about yourself and others? What if, instead of trying to escape this part of your life, you surrendered to it?

Practice this self-acceptance meditation. Get comfortable in a place where you won't be disturbed. Close your eyes, relax your shoulders, and allow your body to settle. Turn your attention to your breathing, and begin inhaling for a count of four to six, and then exhale for a count of four to eight. Continue with this breathing for a few minutes until you feel relaxed. Place your hands over your heart, and repeat the affirmation "I completely love, accept, and forgive myself" aloud. Keep repeating this powerful statement until you no longer feel any resistance.

I welcome freedom and I relinquish control

Learning to trust in something greater than yourself might trigger a fear response from your inner child. It can seem scary to surrender to a higher power.

How does your inner child feel about the possibility of letting go and trusting more? How can you comfort and reassure your inner child about making these changes?

When I trust the process, things fall into place effortlessly

Have you ever had something fall into place without much effort or planning? It almost seems too good to be true, but you feel so fortunate that things have turned out this way. This is the power of surrender.

What is the most wonderful thing you can imagine to happen in your life in the next twelve months? What limiting beliefs would you have to let go of in order to make this thing a reality?

I place my faith in my higher self, allowing it to show me the way

I believe we can all access a higher way of thinking. You might like to call it your intuition, higher self, inner wisdom, or anything else that resonates. This voice might be quiet at first, but the more we tune into it, the stronger it becomes.

What message does your higher self have for you today?

My life is so much easier when I choose to go with the flow

Life is already complicated enough without having to resist everything. Learning to flow with wherever life takes us means we enjoy the journey while feeling peaceful.

Complete this sentence: I know I can handle whatever life throws at me because . . .

It is safe for me to let go of control

Feeling in control gives us a false sense of security. It might seem safer to hold on to everything tightly and keep a watchful eye on things, but in reality, there are way too many aspects at play that it's impossible to control, plan, and predict everything. Sometimes the tighter we cling, the worse it is when things don't go as we expected.

In what areas of your life are you exhibiting too much control?

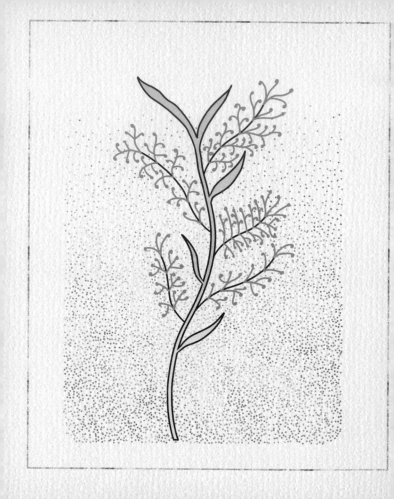

Support, guidance, and assistance are always available to me

Change can be scary, and you don't have to do this alone. Don't hesitate to reach out to your support network when you need it. If you need impartial and anonymous support, there are many wonderful organizations available.

Do you feel any resistance in reaching out for help and support? If you do, use your journal to explore why you might be experiencing this. If you don't, consider writing a thank you note to those in your support network.

Change
empowers me

I believe that real change comes from small, consistent daily actions. As you begin to make micro changes in your daily life, you'll soon notice a big impact on your overall well-being.

What are three things you could change about your daily routine that would bring more ease and flow to your day?

As I let go of what I think is best for me, even more wonderful things enter my life

Some of life's greatest gifts are completely unexpected and it would be impossible to predict them. The more you surrender to the flow of life and the magic it contains, the more life can surprise you.

Take note of your life over the past six to twelve months. What great things happened that were unexpected? If you can't think of anything, what great things do you hope will happen in the next six to twelve months?

I know I will always be held and supported

Having others hold and support you feels good, and we should be grateful for the support that surrounds us, but you are more than capable of holding and supporting yourself too. You always have the option to make time for self-care and engage in activities that make you feel calmer and more balanced.

Who do you rely on for support? Why do you think this is? Is it possible for you to support yourself more?

I will allow life to surprise me

No matter how hard we try, we can't predict the future. We can shape our lives in a certain way in the hopes of creating the best possible outcome, but it's also exciting to think where life might lead us unexpectedly.

What do you intuitively feel about the direction your life might be taking? What might you learn along the way?

I trust my intuition to guide me toward optimal growth

Growth is going to look and feel different for everyone, as we are all walking our own unique paths. Think about what you want to move toward and away from.

Write down three words that define what optimal growth means to you.

I see life as a beautiful journey that I am grateful to be experiencing

At the end of the day, no matter what you're going through or what you're experiencing, life is a beautiful gift. Perspective is everything. We are here by some miracle for an amount of time that no one can say for sure. Let's enjoy every moment.

Journal about a recent moment that made you realize the beauty of life.

Just like a river, I flow with ease

Nature is constantly teaching us lessons. Great power and force can be found in things that often seem calm on the surface. A single drop of water soon accumulates into a river, unstoppable in its force.

Spend some time near water today. Whether you're near the sea, a river, or even a local lake or pond, take time to observe how the water ripples and flows. Or, alternatively, spend some time listening to the sounds of the sea, or go to sleep to the sounds of the ocean.

I surrender my emotions, allowing them to ebb and flow like the tide

Emotions aren't good or bad—they simply are. If you're sensitive, like me, you probably experience emotions very acutely and try to push them away rather than feel their intensity. Making friends with all your emotions takes time, but it's a worthwhile skill to cultivate.

What emotions do you feel the least uncomfortable experiencing and why do you think this is?

I invite calmness into every aspect of my being

We can take lots of positive steps toward becoming a calmer person, and we can also step back and allow calmness to gently come to us, without force or pressure. Some things take time, and that's okay. Don't rush the process.

What would it take for you to fully invite calmness into your life and trust that life is unfolding exactly as it is meant to?

I aim for inner peace rather than perfection

High standards are important, but have you set them so high that no one, including you, will ever be able to meet them? No one or thing is perfect, and it's much better to aim for feelings of contentment rather than perfection. Don't sacrifice your inner peace for something you'll never be able to meet.

What standards are you holding yourself to that you know you will never be able to meet?

I know that everything will unfold exactly as it is meant to

Do you find yourself constantly searching for answers, grasping at making sense of things as soon as you can and looking for a solution as quickly as possible? We all do this, thinking it will help, but sometimes it creates even more uneasiness.

On a piece of paper, write down everything that is currently on your mind that you can't seem to find a solution for. Once you have finished writing, find a place where you can safely burn the paper, signifying that you are now surrendering these thoughts and feelings. Know that you are placing your trust in something bigger, and the solutions will come forward.

I view all experiences as lessons that guide me back toward inner peace

What if everything you experience, no matter how good or bad, has the opportunity to guide you back toward your true self, restore inner peace, and teach you something about what serenity truly is?

Think of an uncomfortable experience that you recently went through. Looking back, what did it teach you about yourself? What can you learn about it that will help you feel calmer and more peaceful moving forward?

I hand over my worries and choose to see the bigger picture

Stress, worry, and anxiety can magnify the problems you're facing, but when you take a step back, you might notice that they aren't as severe as you previously thought. Choose to let them go from your mind, and focus on your life as a whole.

Try this zoom-out technique. Choose one thought/ feeling/event that's prominent in your life right now. Will this thing matter by the end of the day, the week, the month, or even the year? Does it really need so much energy? Of course, things will happen that might have a huge impact, but most of the time we come to realize later on that our current worries weren't as important as we thought.

I trust that this part of my life will provide me with valuable lessons

With a little self-reflection and willingness to think critically, you might find some pretty valuable lessons right before your eyes.

Take note of where you are right now in these areas of your life: health, finances, career, romantic relationships, family and friends, fun and enjoyment, and personal growth. Based on what you have written down, what is each area currently trying to teach you?

I am ready to become the most balanced, peaceful, and calmest version of myself

Your potential is unlimited. Making space for who you might become is scary, but also very exciting. When you feel balanced and grounded within yourself, your whole life will change to reflect this back to you.

Complete this sentence: When I finally let go of everything I think I should be, I create the space to become . . .

Library of Congress Cataloging-in-Publication Data

Names: Trewick, Elicia Rose, author.
Title: Calm: 100 affirmations for serenity
    / Elicia Rose Trewick, Creator of Bloom Affirmations.
Other titles: Calm: a hundred affirmations for serenity
Description: New York, NY : Rock Point, 2022. | Series: Inspiring guides |
    Summary: "Feeling calm and at ease is made easy and simple with Calm:
    100 Affirmations for Serenity, your peaceful ritual filled with affirmations and
    guided prompts to help you achieve personal growth"—Provided by publisher.
Identifiers: LCCN 2021061805 (print) | LCCN 2021061806 (ebook) | ISBN
    9781631068645 (hardcover) | ISBN 9780760376324 (ebook)
Subjects: LCSH: Calmness. | Mindfulness (Psychology) | Affirmations. | Self-
    actualization (Psychology)
Classification: LCC BF575.C35 T74 2022 (print) | LCC BF575.C35 (ebook) |
    DDC 158.1--dc23/eng/20220211
LC record available at https://lccn.loc.gov/2021061805
LC ebook record available at https://lccn.loc.gov/2021061806

Publisher: Rage Kindelsperger   Editor: Keyla Pizarro-Hernández
Creative Director: Laura Drew   Cover and Interior Design: Amy Sly
Managing Editor: Cara Donaldson

About the
Author

Elicia Rose is a writer and illustrator based in Sheffield, England. She is the creator of Bloom Affirmations. What originally began as an Instagram page trying to make social media a kinder place to be has bloomed into an array of work focused on helping people feel better about themselves through the power of positive affirmations and journaling. Find out more at bloomaffirmations.com